Written by **Rebekah Paster**

SUPER-ish FRIENDS

Illustrated by **Gin Tran**

Written by **Rebekah Paster**

Illustrated by **Gin Tran**

Hardcover ISBN: 979-8-9942041-0-8

Paperback ISBN: 979-8-9942041-1-5

For more information, visit *superishfriends.com*

For my dad,
my first and forever hero.

For my husband,
my steady strength and greatest teammate.

For my boys, Gavin and Jackson,
my brightest lights and biggest adventures.

And for anyone who has ever felt different — put on your cape,
stand tall, and remember:
the world needs you just as you are.

Winnie woke up as the sun crept into her window. She sat up in bed and stretched her arms.

Well, her one arm.

Today is the big obstacle course at school, and as Winnie thought about it, her tummy did a little flip. All of the kids would be running, climbing ropes, and swinging from the monkey bars.

Winnie had only one hand, and she wasn't sure she could do it all.

As she stood in front of the mirror, she looked down at
her missing hand. Her mom always called it her "mighty
hand," but this morning, it felt more like a "maybe" hand.

Just then, Winnie's mom peeked into her room.

"Are you ready for the big day?"
she asked.

Winnie frowned a little. "I guess,
but what if I can't do it, Mom?
What if they all laugh at me
because I'm different?"

Her mom walked over
and hugged Winnie.

"Different? That just
means you're awesome
in a new way."

"I wear glasses - remember the time I sat on them and wore the lenses taped to a spoon?" Winnie giggled.

"You, my dear, have your mighty hand!"

"Everyone has something that makes them special."

When Winnie got to school that morning, the playground was super busy!

The kids were running, laughing and practicing for the big day.

She spotted her friend Ava,
whose face was sprinkled
with freckles.

Ava was smiling and
ready for the day.

"Hey, Winnie!" Ava waved. "Are you ready for the obstacle course? It's going to be so much fun!"

Winnie waved back but still felt a little nervous.
"I don't know, Ava. What if I mess up because
I'm different, and everyone laughs at me?"

Ava shook her head and pointed to her freckles.
"No way! My freckles may be different, but I love them!

My mom calls them my magic spots. You've got your own magic, too — you'll see!"

Winnie lined up with her classmates at the start of the obstacle course.

First, they had to run through some tires.

Winnie ran as fast as she could, her feet landing in just the right spots.

Next up was the balance beam.
Winnie watched Ava, full of
determination, walk across with ease.

"FRECKLE POWER!" laughed Ava as she carefully reached the other side of the beam.

Winnie was amazed by her friend's confidence. Ava loved her freckles, even though kids used to ask her why she had so many.

But now, Ava brushes it off, calling them her **"magic spots."**

When it was Winnie's turn, she realized she could do this, too. As she made her way across the beam, Winnie used her mighty hand to keep steady.

"I knew you could do it!" said Ava. "Next up, monkey bars!"

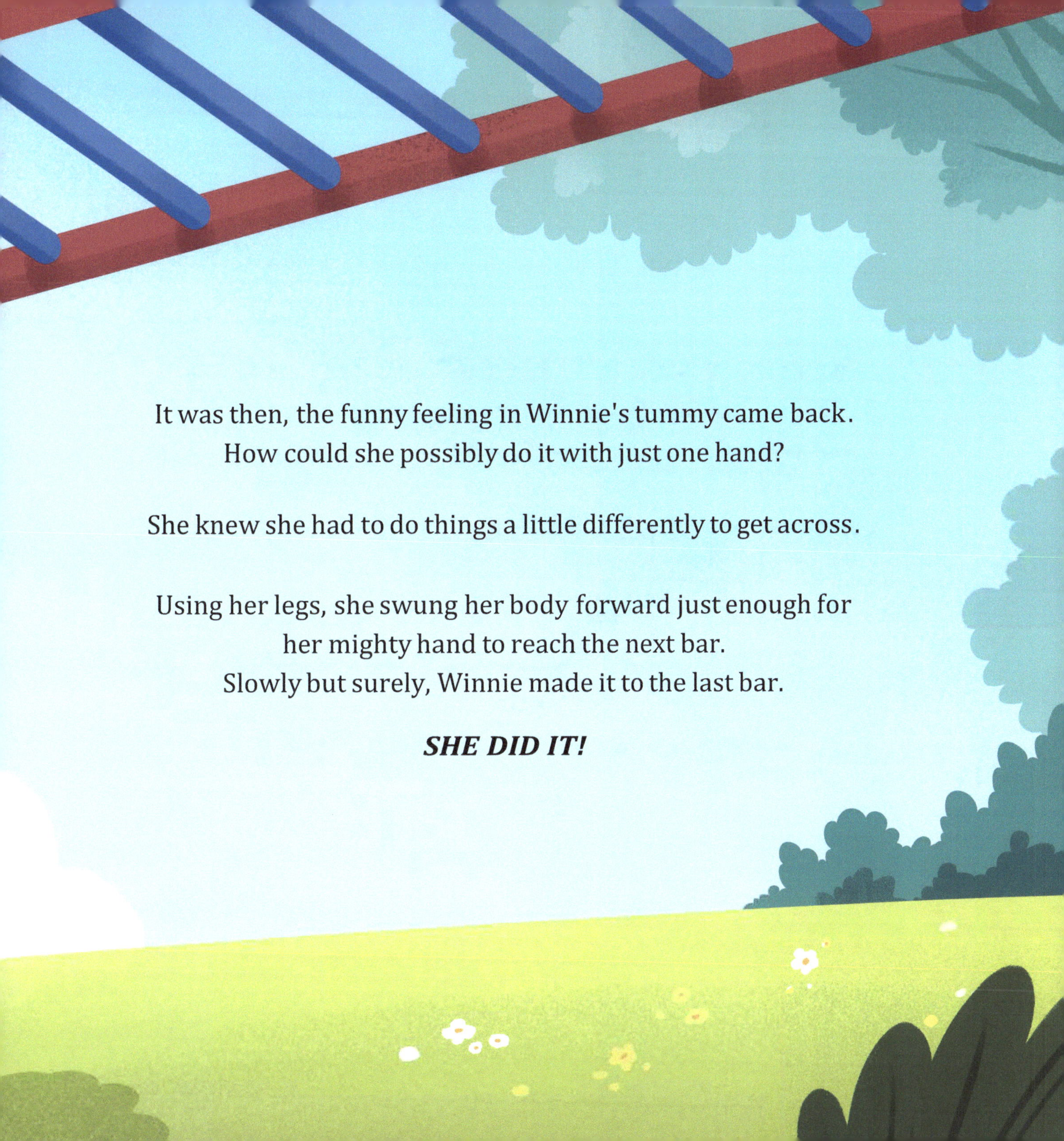

It was then, the funny feeling in Winnie's tummy came back.
How could she possibly do it with just one hand?

She knew she had to do things a little differently to get across.

Using her legs, she swung her body forward just enough for
her mighty hand to reach the next bar.
Slowly but surely, Winnie made it to the last bar.

SHE DID IT!

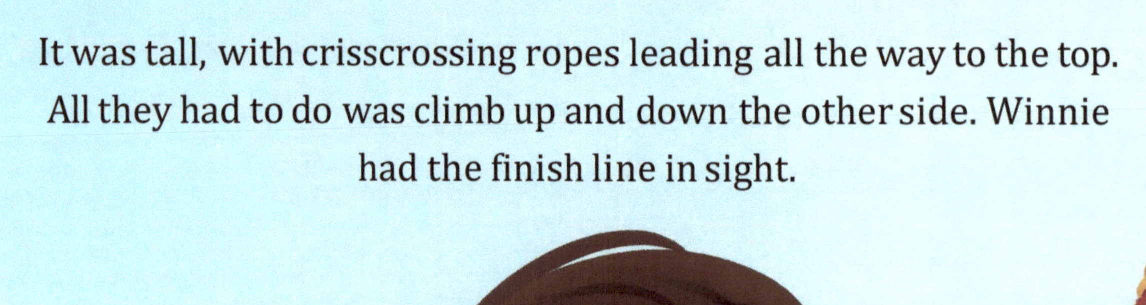

After Winnie's big victory on the monkey bars, they
moved onto the final challenge - the rope wall.

It was tall, with crisscrossing ropes leading all the way to the top.
All they had to do was climb up and down the other side. Winnie
had the finish line in sight.

Winnie's friend, Charlie, took a deep breath and adjusted his glasses.
"I think I can spot the best path with my super glasses," he said, squinting
at the ropes.

"Good eye!" called Ava.
"Freckle power and super glasses to the rescue!"

As Winnie grabbed onto the first
rope, she knew she'd have to climb
differently than the others, but this
didn't bother her anymore.

Just as Winnie did on the monkey bars, she used her strong legs to push herself up one knot at a time.

With each knot she climbed, she felt stronger and more confident in finishing the obstacle course.

She had done it! She climbed the rope wall like her friends, but in her own special way.

As Winnie, Ava and Charlie crossed the finish line together,
Mrs. Marine stood and greeted them with a big smile.
"Great job, team!" she said.

"You all finished the course using your own special way to do it!"

As they all smiled and celebrated the big
victory together, Winnie felt happier —
and relieved — *more than ever.*

She knew whatever challenges came her way,
she could always find her way through it.
Being different wasn't something to fear.

It was something to be proud of.

About the Author

Rebekah Paster is a mom, storyteller, and dreamer who believes the most powerful thing you can be is yourself. As one of the first models with a limb difference to walk in New York Fashion Week, she continues to inspire others through her writing and advocacy.

She is passionate about giving back and proudly supports organizations such as Lucky Fin Project and Ed Snider Youth Hockey & Education, both dedicated to empowering children through inclusion, confidence, and teamwork.

About Lucky Fin Project

Lucky Fin Project 501(c)(3) is a nonprofit organization that exists to raise awareness and celebrate children, individuals, and families affected by limb differences (upper, lower, congenital, and amputee).

What they do:
- Creates a support network for parents across the U.S. and around the world.
- Links parents to medical information and resources.
- Provides education on limb differences.
- Hosts events and financially support efforts for children to attend specialized camps, obtain prosthetics, and to fund other organizations within the limb different community.

9 789899 420411 5